College Essay Insider Secrets

How to write a killer essay for the 2017-2018 Common Application that puts your best foot forward, tells your unique story and multiplies your odds of admission to the most competitive colleges in the country

Andy Lockwood

With Sarah Idzik

Table Of Contents

FREE UPDATES AND WEBCLASS

This book is only part of the story about what it REALLY takes to get into - and pay "wholesale" prices for - the best colleges in the country. For learn how to multiply your odds of admission and fat, juicy scholarships, visit:

www.CollegeAdmissionsWebcast.com

Forward

Why this college essay book is different

According to a study (the two second Google search I just did[1]), there are 75,400,000 mentions of "college essay book" on the Internet.

So why did I add to this mess?

Because, no matter how much "new" information is published (some very good books, by the way) each and every summer in my college admissions and financial aid consulting practice, we see, up close and personal, scores of families who are ridiculously stressed and uptight about the d-mn essay!

Or essays, I should say.

Some kids write 10,15, even 30 or more essays for college! The grand total depends on the schools they're applying to, and of course how many colleges are on the final list.

That's why I say that the college essay is approximately one part writing ability and two parts time management. Sooner or later, kids run out of time.

Now (2017) that the choices on the Common Application changed, I figured it was time to step in and help kids get through the process as quickly and easily as possible.

---

[1] MAN am I exhausted!

If you're like most kids or parents[2] about to tackle the college applications and essays, you undoubtedly have a bunch of questions, such as:

Do admissions officers actually read the essays?

If so, how much weight do they attribute to them in the overall admissions application?

What are "good" topics? Bad ones?

What mistakes should you avoid at all costs?

Is it OK to talk about a learning disability or other issue?

What about political topics - are they OK to write about or should you avoid them like tickets to the next "Kars For Kids" concert?[3]

What Works In College Essays, Here On Planet Earth

If you have any of these questions, this book is for you. Inside, you will NOT find vague theory or half-baked opinions that have no basis in reality.

The "bones" of this book are based on an interview I conducted with a friend and colleague, Sarah Idzik, former admissions officer at The University Of Chicago.

Why should you care about her credentials? U Chicago has an

---

[2] I mean "moms."

[3] Dude, I saw them in Aspen in '89 - they were AWESOME!

admissions rate around 7% and is known for its esoteric supplemental essays. Sarah spent five years and read close to 1,000 applications per year! She now works one-on-one with our clients, especially those applying to Ivy League and other competitive colleges.

If anyone is qualified to tell you *exactly* what an admissions office is hoping to read - and what NOT to read - in an essay, it's Sarah.

Most kids and parents don't have the opportunity that you hold in your hands. They solicit advice from their English teachers, guidance counselors, other parents and kids.

Let me be blunt: if you do this, your results will be, at best, hit and miss. Please contemplate these experts' credentials and, at the very least, take their advice with a grain of salt or three.

You shouldn't have to work too hard to get the value out of this book. I attempted to write it in a conversational style, not a dry textbook. You should be able to get through it in one or two sittings, either in a traditional, upholstered chair or perhaps one of the porcelain variety.[4]

WARNING, there are a few jokes sprinkled throughout this book. Maybe more than a few. If you don't like "funny" or you would rather be MORE stressed out about the college essays, please stop reading and give this book to another parent, kid, or random guy under a bridge.

Final comment: I decided to keep this book short because I'd rather you spend your time thinking, drafting and editing your essays, instead

---

[4] Classy!

of getting bogged down and confounded by contradictory half-baked opinions and "alternative facts" spouted out by folks who really have no basis for doing so.

So grab your highlighter, your favorite beverage and let's dig in!

Chapter 1

Know Your Audience

Yes, the essay is about YOU, but check your narcissism at the door for a few moments and think about whom you're writing FOR.

Imagine the life of an admissions officer, who has several hundred applications to read in a matter of weeks. Imagine further that most of the applicants have substantially the same GPA's and test scores, glowing teacher recommendations and activity sheets bursting up to the eyeballs with "leadership" and "enrichment" activities!

(Side note: apparently only "leaders" apply to college, there are no followers. If you read as many applications as I do, this is the only reasonable conclusion. :)

Seriously, if you're an admissions officer, how are you supposed to select the applicants who belong at your college?

The personal statement, or college essay, is one of the most direct ways for applicants to proffer their case why they deserve to be considered.

Put another way, the essay can help a college applicant explain *I know that I have the same grades and test scores as 5,000 of my competitors, but THIS is why you should take ME!*

In the interview that follows, former admissions officer Sarah Idzik freely admits that she and her fellow admissions officers are human

9

beings - they, like you and I, fall prey to different moods when they read applications and essays.

Naturally, you don't want your admissions officer to be bored or frustrated when she starts reading your essay. How do you prevent this?

It's not always by writing a catchy introduction, although that can help grab attention. (One of my all-time faves, *So there I was, three years after my bar mitzvah, about to receive communion, and...* How can you NOT want to continue reading that one?)

It's more about telling the reader what she's going to get out of reading your essay. The benefit or the promise you're making to them up front.

You have a maximum of 650 words, which means that you must cut to the chase quickly. No meandering!

On that note, it's only appropriate for us to get right to the 2017-2018 Common Application Essay Prompts! (Yay.)

FREE Companion Webinar

What does it really take to get into a top college (hint: it's NOT only about grades and SAT/ACT scores). We run free webinars on college admissions and scholarships strategies 1-2x per month.
To see our upcoming schedule, visit:

www.CollegeAdmissionsWebcast.com

Chapter 2

The 2017-2018 Common Application Essay Prompts

The folks at the Common App change their essay "prompts," or questions, every so often. This year (2017), they tweaked the ones that they put in place two years prior.

Although you have different choices, the prompts are so open-ended that you have a ton of room to say whatever it is you want to get across about yourself. (On a related note, the prompts' open-endedness is a big reason why Sarah and I think the new, last choice - write whatever the hell you want to write - will almost never be necessary and should be avoided.)

If you read the choices and feel frustrated or confused, don't worry, you're not alone. Seriously, it's like you're being asked, *Here are a bunch of cliche questions...write a non-cliche answer!*

But that's just my opinion, I'm easily irritated.

These questions are different than the types of writing assignments English teachers give in high school. They demand more personal reflection.

They're not creative writing exercises, research papers or other formal assignments, either.

Let's take a look at the actual prompts and think about how you'd answer each. It's entirely possible that one of them will leap out at you as The One, but it's perfectly natural if your first reaction is *I have no clue how to answer any of them!*

If you have the latter reaction, by the time you read through my interview with Sarah, at the very least you'll be at the point of saying, *I guess "this one" sucks less than the others.*

Hey, I'll take it! :)

Here's the whole list. Buzz through them, but don't get too hung up. In the next few chapters, we'll go through each one.

1. Some students have a background, identity, interest, or talent that is so meaningful they believe their application would be incomplete without it. If this sounds like you, then please share your story.

2. The lessons we take from obstacles we encounter can be fundamental to later success. Recount a time when you faced a challenge, setback, or failure. How did it affect you, and what did you learn from the experience?

3. Reflect on a time when you questioned or challenged a belief or idea. What prompted your thinking? What was the outcome?

4. Describe a problem you've solved or a problem you'd like to solve. It can be an intellectual challenge, a research query, an ethical dilemma - anything that is of personal importance, no matter the scale. Explain its significance to you and what steps you took or could be taken to identify a solution.

5. Discuss an accomplishment, event, or realization that sparked a period of personal growth and a new understanding of yourself or others.

6. Describe a topic, idea, or concept you find so engaging that it makes you lose all track of time. Why does it captivate you? What or who do you turn to when you want to learn more?

7. Share an essay on any topic of your choice. It can be one you've already written, one that responds to a different prompt, or one of your own design.

Alrighty, let's take a closer look at Prompt 1...

Chapter 3

Prompt 1

Some students have a background, identity, interest, or talent that is so meaningful they believe their application would be incomplete without it. If this sounds like you, then please share your story.

Following is a (somewhat cleaned up) transcription of my interview with Sarah Idzik, drawing on her five years' experience as an admissions officer at the University Of Chicago.

Andy: Alright Sarah, what are your thoughts on the first essay prompt?

Sarah: I'm going to say this first, then I'll say some nicer things that will not sound as harsh, but I want to get this out of the way.

Remember that a lot of things, or qualities or experiences, these things they're listing, background, identity, interest or talent, can sound or be truly unique in isolation, but massed together with a pile of 30,000 other applicants, might not necessarily be. The key is not just the "thing" (background, identity, etc.). This fact in isolation doesn't really mean anything.

What really gives it life is the way it fits into your life or your personality or your experiences, your way of seeing the world, your own background. That's what the question is actually asking. This has to be about your story, not just about this one isolated fact. Don't assume that the fact or the talent alone will speak for itself.

A lot of people play musical instruments or play sports or ride horses or whatever it is the case may be. It's really more about your experience in your life, so make it personal. You have to really take the chance to make it personal, otherwise it'll come off as kind of generic no matter how awesome the thing itself is. It could be the "awesomest" thing in the world and you could still write a really bland essay about it.

It's always so important to pay attention to the language of the prompt itself and think about what it's REALLY asking. This one asks about a background, identity, or talent, but then literally says "share your story." It's asking you to do both, so you have to be responsible for doing both.

Keep in mind that admissions counselors are trying to build a community of people who interact in a lot of different ways and not just in the classroom. Yes, they're looking at facts in a sense that it would be cool to have a student from all 50 states, if possible, or from a lot of different countries or students with different majors or areas of interest, but also just knowing who you are and what matters to you will give them a sense of how you might be involved in life when you get on campus and whether that fills a niche that they want or need, or whether that suits the personality of the institution itself.

Another really important thing for this prompt is that it's asking for something that's actually meaningful to you personally, not just like a standard impressive fact. Not just what you think that we or they want to hear. Truly, truly, truly, anything can actually fit the bill.

In some ways the question is actually a little bit misleading because I would argue that probably everybody has something that is special enough that they want to write about in this prompt. I think it can be something as big as, "I competed in the junior Olympics," or something as small as, "I cook dinner for my family three times a week and it's this really special time that we all have together and we've carved that out in our lives and I'm really glad that I can make that happen." The scope and the scale is not what really makes the difference here. What makes the difference is how you talk about it.

Lastly, it's better to choose something that isn't already thoroughly represented in the rest of the app to avoid too much repetition, and of course to avoid vagueness, generality, and clichés.

Andy: If you're too vague, does that show a lack of thought?

Sarah: I think it's really more the lack of engagement. Because a lot of students writing these types of essays can mean well or have intentions to engage more deeply, but if the effect is vague and general, the reader is going to see something that doesn't tell you anything about the student, first of all, and also suggests that maybe the student was a little too afraid to take the chance to be more personal. If there's ever going to be a time to get personal, that time is now on this essay prompt.

I think what's hard about that is that this is not really a way that anyone is used to writing. It's a really niche kind of writing style, a genre in and of itself. It's not something that you learn in school when you're writing for Honors English or AP English or something. These are not the essays that you're writing.

This is really more like it's first-person, but not just straight, dry, autobiographical--it's also storytelling. It's nonfiction storytelling. It's like a storytelling slam but on paper and for higher stakes. I think often times the tendency is to sort of step back and write in more vague, mannered language to sidestep the challenge of that and the fear that you're going to be judged, but the whole point of this is to be judged.

Not necessarily in a negative way, but you have to give us something to be able to judge, otherwise you can't make the decision if you're reading it. You just don't know who that person is.

Andy: Right there, covering only one out of seven prompts, Sarah gave a seminar in and of itself. One of my key takeaways is "Don't be afraid of going small." You contrasted a kid who's writing about being a junior Olympic athlete versus someone who cooks dinner for their family. I think a lot of the more interesting essays are about the small things.

Tip: You don't need to write about a grand idea or monumental experience (i.e., use excessive artistic license or, let's face it, lie). It's perfectly OK to "go small."

18

Chapter 4

Prompt 2

The lessons we take from obstacles we encounter can be fundamental to later success. Recount a time when you faced a challenge, setback or failure. How did it affect you and how did you learn from this experience?

Andy: I want to just narrow the scope a little bit, because sometimes kids try to make a mountain out of a molehill answering this prompt.

They talk about some huge obstacle - to THEM - that's not really so big (like the time they gave the wrong answer in class). In contrast, in the above discussion you spoke of "going small", so I can see two paths to take here. What are your thoughts on this prompt?

Sarah: Yeah, I'm glad you brought that up because that was one of my first thoughts. They changed the language a little bit in this prompt from last year because instead of obstacles, I think it just said failure. "Lessons we take from failures," which is strongly worded and I think drove people to think more in terms of these really stark, big moments in their lives.

I think this change helps a little bit by saying "obstacles." It guides you towards a more broad definition of what that might mean. I do think that again, what you define as an obstacle, a challenge, a setback or failure can be extremely broad.

A lot of people do tend and did tend to go with academic or extracurricular failures. A lot of like, "I choked at the big recital" and examples like that. I read a lot of those. Lots of different instruments and different ways to choke at recitals out there. Not that that can't be told in an interesting way, but you do see it a lot. I think that's a more obvious way to take the prompt. But you don't have to, it does not have to be something that was at school where everyone saw you, or in your broader community or, like, you ran for student body president and you didn't get it. I mean, that might have happened to you, but that doesn't happen to everybody, right? It could be something within your own household.

I remember reading an essay on this prompt about an issue between that person and one other person, a friend. It could also be something within yourself. I think opening that up and thinking a little bit more creatively is going to help you because if everybody's writing about these big moments, like "I choked during the big X thing," and you're writing about something that's really different, still within the parameters of the prompt, but something smaller or more personal, that's going to be different than everyone else which makes you stand out and be more memorable.

I think the temptation to go with the more obvious, big moment is actually a little bit of an obstacle itself, you might say, insofar as it's a lot more likely to have been told before in some form.

However, if you take a smaller, more intimate approach, it's a lot less likely to have been talked about by thousands of other essay writers in the past. That's really what you want, right? You want originality, you want to show creativity in the sense that it seems original in the true sense of the word. You're the only person who could have written this

22

essay in this way.

Andy: Sorry to interrupt.[5] So when you're at the University of Chicago admissions office, and there's 30,000 applications per year, and you read 1,000 or whatever yourself, I imagine that the vast majority of them are these uber-competitive, super smart kids who are nearly perfect on paper.

Sarah: Yeah.

Andy: Can this "setback or failure" essay be used to humanize kids a little bit?

Sarah: Absolutely, and it really does work that way. That's another good point too, I think: it's easy to get caught up in your own impact as an individual in your life, in your school community, but depending on the tier of school or the level of selectivity of the school you're applying to, yeah, UChicago, there were a lot, a lot of applicants like that. To a certain degree, that high level of achievement, being shown to you again and again and again can actually get kind of monotonous. This prompt does work to humanize an applicant, absolutely. If there is a memorable or a touching or an interesting or a curious personal story, it sticks with you.

Andy: When we were chatting offline before, I was saying something like when I read four essays in a row I'm exhausted. I can't imagine what it was like for you plowing through 1,000 applications each year.

I'm imagining that at some point, you're practically begging someone

---

[5] I wasn't really THAT sorry.

to tell you something interesting or humanizing. Is that true?

Sarah: At UChicago I became trained to see every potential response to the Extended Essay prompts. You read them and immediately anticipate how it can be turned into the generic version that you'll see 700 times.

So it's big deal when you read an essay that you didn't predict you'd get! To me, that's the key, because everybody is different and unique and interesting, and if you tell your story, and are true to that story, it should itself be different and unique and interesting. I shouldn't be able to predict what you're going to tell me.

Andy: What about if someone had an obstacle or setback that involved some kind of ethical issue, an arrest, cheating or something along those lines? Is that something to stay away from, or is it something that can be handled the right way?

Sarah: This can definitely be handled the right way. First off, in the Common Application, if you have been convicted of a crime or have been suspended from school, that will have to be divulged anyway, so we'll see that. There's a space to provide an explanation and you have to do that.

Andy: Right. What if it doesn't rise to that level though? What if it's something that did not have to be disclosed that way?

Sarah: Right. It's something you can write about and you can write about it well. I would just be very careful about how you do that and couch it appropriately. If it's something that you were questioning and you feel like from a moral standpoint this was important to you and no one got hurt in the end, then I think that's okay as long as you tell it fairly and kind of generously.

However, if it was kind of ethically questionable or potentially harmful to other people, and that question doesn't resolve by the end of the story, I would perhaps not write that because anything that might result in harm to others is something that admissions will flag because we don't want to potentially invite this person to our campus where they might hurt someone in some way.

Andy: From a legal standpoint, imagine if a college admitted someone they knew was a risk to others, and then that student ultimately hurt someone else once they got to campus. The college would be accused of being liable by the victim's attorneys.

Tip: Don't write about the voices in your head or talk about how you like to run over other people's toes with your dad's car. Any disability you choose to write about should not be a lurking liability for a college that admits you.

Chapter 5

Prompt 3

Reflect on a time when you questioned or challenged a belief or idea. What prompted your thinking? What was the outcome?

Andy: I kind of like this one a lot.

Sarah: Yeah, I really like this one a lot too. I like this question because it's asking multiple questions. Again, it's important to focus on all the different parts of that process and pay close attention to the language of the prompt. If you really attend to that language, it'll tell you that it wants 1. a particular descriptive experience, 2. what precipitated it, and 3. what you did with it. You really want to make sure you get all three pieces of that.

What I like about this is that it shows an interest in your, the applicant's, capacity to think in complex and multi-sided or multi-dimensional ways, which is I think a sign of intellectual growth as you go through your young adult life. Going from thinking about things in more one-dimensional or binary ways, to thinking in shades of gray. I think that's really what this question is asking. How did that process begin with you? When did you start developing the ability to think critically or independently? How does this fit into that story?

If you don't have a way to answer this that's obvious to you, then you don't have to answer it, but that is I think a good way to show that you're starting to think more in a college level way.

You don't necessarily want this to be a sermon, like a moralizing or a judging response. Obviously, challenging something requires judgment, so it means that you were thinking for yourself and judging that something needed to be questioned. That's really good, just be careful in the way that you talk about it.

Just thinking about your audience, and knowing that your admissions counselor who's reading it, or counselors, can be anyone from any kind of background, any school of belief. They could be conservative, they could be liberal, they could be religious, they could be not, and so on. In the way that the college, the admissions office wants to see that you're thinking critically, they also want to see that you're thinking generously. So that if they were to admit you and you got to their campus, you would be able to voice an opinion about something in class discussion, but you would also be really mindful of what other people had to say.

I think that's a little bit of the trick with this question. If you do it well, you can really show a lot of nuance.

Andy: That answer ties into a question that was submitted ahead of time by our client Hilit, who had asked about politics and this crazy times, and I think your answer, not to put words in your mouth, is probably along the lines of "that's okay as long as you're not being too over the top or doctrinaire, and you show that you're open to other ideas but you at the same time expressed how you stood up for your beliefs."

Sarah: Yeah, exactly. I would imagine that this prompt might draw out some essays about politics. If you have a family whose political views are opposed to yours, for instance.. I think there's absolutely a way to write about it, but non-sanctimoniously, non-self-righteously.

Andy: So don't cut and paste a Facebook post?

Sarah: Yeah, exactly. Nothing inspired by a meme. Something that shows a little bit of nuance, and ideally a recognition that these issues are a little bit complex.

Maybe the thing that you question has merits of its own, but in the end, after you weighed that and you really thought about it, you decided that even despite that, you still thought it should be challenged. Or you might say that yeah, okay, your relatives might support the candidate that you don't, but they're still people and you still love them, they still have things that they really care about and believe. I think showing that you think through those kinds of things and nuances is going to show that you're really ready for college-level thinking. And life.

Andy: What's really interesting is that, recently (2017) there have been all sorts of speakers scheduled to speak at campuses but they weren't allowed on campus because of protests. Is it really that different for admissions officers?

Sarah: Yeah, that's a really good question because it's an interesting, very complicated, always-shifting dynamic on college campuses. At UChicago, it's a really politically active campus. There's a lot of student activism happening all the time around various issue. In the admissions office I think you're sort of part of the institution. You represent the institution, so I would not have associated the admissions office itself with that kind of really strong student activism that was happening on the student side on campus. We had to be more ideologically neutral.

I think that admissions officers definitely represent different beliefs and perspectives, but in the end it's really more about putting together the right kind of class for the school. So for instance, if I worked at UC Berkeley, an institution that basically defined college student activism, and I'm reading applications and I come across someone who says, "I hate student activism." That's an exaggeration, but you know...

Andy: What if they say, "I love Donald Trump and every conservative person and I'm pro ... I'm anti ..." I don't know, whatever.

Sarah: Something that we used to say all the time was to be really careful to check your biases as an application reader. Obviously, there are things that you kind of gravitate towards and react against innately just because of your own leanings. I think in that case actually, you would almost be trained to say to yourself, okay, I don't want to react against this person because they believe the opposite of what I believe. I want to give them all due consideration, as long as what this person is saying is not like, "I don't want to go to a college with a single person who doesn't support Donald Trump."

I think in an ideal world, what colleges want to do is create an environment where people with different viewpoints actually can come together and have civil conversation.

Tip: It's OK to talk about your political or other touchy beliefs as long as you demonstrate that you THOUGHT about, and acknowledged the other side. The essay is not the place to "go extreme."

FREE UPDATES AND WEBCLASS ON "The Rest of The Story"

This book is only part of the story about what it REALLY takes to get into - and pay "wholesale" prices for - the best colleges in the country. For learn how to multiply your odds of admission and fat, juicy scholarships, visit:

www.CollegeAdmissionsWebcast.com

Chapter 6

Prompt 4

Describe a problem you've solved or a problem you'd like to solve. It can be an intellectual challenge, a research query, an ethical dilemma. Anything that is of personal importance, no matter the scale. Explain its significance to you and what steps you took or could be taken to identify a solution.

Andy: That's a mouthful.

Sarah: It is a mouthful. I think it's maybe the toughest one and probably the one last year that I saw the least when I was reading. It probably appeals a little bit more towards problem-solving thinkers, people who are a little bit more research-oriented, but it does not have to be science-related or STEM-related in any way. You can really address a wide range of things with this question--notice that it says "no matter the scale"--, but I think the key, because it's worded a little bit impersonally, is not to fall into a style of writing that is impersonal.

Andy: Yeah.

Sarah: You're not writing a lab report. You want to still be able to tell a story and connect it to your own experience. Thinking about whatever this problem was that you've solved, okay, so you solved it, or you didn't solve it, so what? That's the question you always want to be asking yourself. How do I tie this into something bigger? What can I say consequentially happened? Did that change my community, or my school, or myself? What resulted from this aside from the fact that I identified a problem and I solved it, and then I moved on with my life. That's not an interesting story.

Andy: Okay, yeah. I've seen a lot of kids tackle it exactly that way and I think the meat is in the turning over the problem, which different ways could you have gone, what were the consequences ... I mean, it's really a window to get to see how you think.

Sarah: Yeah, exactly. The "so what" can mean a lot of different things. That could be like, "so I really enjoy thinking about things this way and therefore I solved the problem this way." That tells us something about how you think. Or, "This kind of problem really matters to me because of this thing in my history or this thing that I really care about and want to do," so that tells us something about you. You just have to connect it and not leave it just isolated, and not just as a throwaway in the last paragraph. Like, "I did this because I want to solve x, y, z disease and because I want to help people."

That's a hot tip. It's great if you want to be a doctor, but everyone says they want to do it because they want to help people, so be more specific if that's the case.

Andy: "I want to help people and I want to make a lot of money."

Sarah: Right.

Andy: Okay, you're in!

Sarah: Oh, that's a new one!

Andy: Yeah, right? It's an honest one.

Tip: Many writers describe the first part, the problem to solve, but fail to explore the "Why." Don't do this (duh). It's the second part of the prompt that lets your admissions officer see what you're all about, beyond grades and standardized test scores..

Chapter 7

Prompt 5

Discuss an accomplishment, event or realization that sparked a period of personal growth and a new understanding of yourself and others.

Andy: (Overly excitedly) That's a new one!

Sarah: Yeah, it's a bit of a word salad, isn't it? The version of this last year was about the accomplishment or event that marked your transition from childhood to adulthood, which I think a lot of people were taking very literally, so maybe that's why they changed the the language a bit.

Andy: Too many bat mitzvah and Quinceañera essays.

Sarah: Exactly, all of that. Those major milestones. I think the key here is that this can be something that is marked by a formal event, like those examples, like a bar mitzvah or bat mitzvah, your first driver's license, or whatever, but it also does not have to be that.

These don't have to be major obvious life milestones. Something that's revelatory in a personal way can also and maybe would also work better. Something that maybe speaks to your powers of reflection, reflecting back on something that happened that you didn't realize at the time was a significant moment, because that doesn't happen to people. You don't think like, this is happening to me right now. Oh my God, I'm transitioning to adulthood as we stand here. That's not real.

It's more like you're reflecting back on something and then you think, yeah, this was something that really changed. Either it really expanded the way that I see the world, it really developed my level of maturity, it changed my relationship with my family or my friends in a certain way.

That's why I kind of like the softened language, because personal growth can mean a lot of different things. So I think maybe what I would recommend if you're approaching this prompt if you have a moment of growth in mind, is to define first what personal growth means to you, even loosely, as it relates to the particular instance or moment of growth that might come to mind for you. How you would define that? Because if you write an entire essay up to the point where you've gotten to the moment where you have to explain, as the prompt asks, the period of personal growth, and you don't really have anything concrete or cohesive or coherent to say about what that actually is to you, I will tell you, if I'm proofreading it with you, I will tell you you need to define personal growth for yourself first before you can really make a coherent case for the fact that this *was* a moment of personal growth.

It doesn't have to be like bullet point list, but you should have an idea of what that means, whether that's a certain world view or a certain kind of maturity or what have you.

The last thing is, it's so hard to say just avoid cliches, but I feel like this one is like begging for it, you know?

Andy: "I made the cheerleading team, even though I was cut the year before."

Sarah: Oh my gosh, I saw so many of those. Yeah. Yeah, lots of failed to make the team and then made the team and then I learned something about myself.

Perseverance is a pretty common theme. Perseverance is a wonderful quality and I know that there are really good ways to write about how you learned it, but in that context you do see it a lot. That's what I'm here to tell you. I'm sorry, but those come up frequently. Try not to be general. If you're going to tell that story, fine, and it can absolutely be done well, but put in as much personal detail as possible.

I found that this year, that was one of the most common pieces of advice I was giving in terms of essay writing and editing and proofreading. I need more detail. I need to know more about how this affected you. How did you feel? What was your response? What did you say? Those things are going to add color even if it's a more cliché story on paper, the shape of it.

Andy: Well I think what makes a cliché question turn not-so-cliché, is if you personalize it and you actually talk about it specifically.

Truthfully, all of these choices are really open-ended, cliché, begging prompts. It's kind of hard to say, "Here's a bunch of cliché prompts. Write me an essay that's not cliché."

Sarah: It's so true. It's true, and I know that's how they're trying to keep it open enough so that they can get all kinds of answers, but I really do think for this one, the key would be to define for yourself before you start writing what that personal growth is, the new understanding of yourself or others. It's almost like you can't really start writing it until you know what that is and how you're going to get there, right?

Tip: Stay away from writing about obvious, common milestones. Think about how you can surprise the reader with a not-so-obvious milestone or event, perhaps one that you did not notice at the time (because it wasn't "obvious" Hello???)

Chapter 8

Prompt 6

Describe a topic, idea or concept you find so engaging that makes you lose all track of time. Why does it captivate you? What or who do you turn to when you want to learn more?

Andy: I like that one.[6]

Sarah: Yeah, this is a totally new one, right? You said that.

Andy: Yeah.

Sarah: Yeah. Yeah, I like this because this is really an invitation to me to "nerd out" as much as possible. I think that something that you see a lot on the college side when you're reading these, or when you're interacting with high school students--or probably you, high school students, feel this yourselves in your own high school environments: it can be a place or kind of an environment where your ability to really nerd out can be kind of dulled or suppressed or repressed in some way just because of the environment and the pressures of being in high school.

When I was in high school I was really, really into Lord of the Rings.

---

[6] Did anyone ask? (Nope.)

Andy: (Snickers audibly)

Sarah: ....but that wasn't really like something you could go around talking about a lot. It's not really until you're an adult that you can really do that. I think this is an invitation for you to really express that. I also think the prompt is asking the "thing" to be something that could potentially have an impact in the world. "Topic idea or concept" can mean anything, but in reality, if you're talking about something that has no bearing on how you interact with the world or other people interact with the world, I don't think it's going to be as interesting an essay.

"Who or what do you turn to when you want to learn more" is a very interesting part of the question. That surprised me. I always really liked reading about kids who were like, "I fell down this Wikipedia hole for half of a day," because that means that you're super curious and you're interested and there aren't things that you're turning your back to because you just think that it's not you.

I think part of why that language is tacked onto this prompt is so that they can see not just, are you really engaged and passionate about something, which is important. You should have something that you're passionate about generally, especially if you're answering this prompt. But it's also if you capable of developing that and linking it to other things.

Learning more, adding onto it, instead of just kind of like weirdly obsessing over one thing: they want to know what you're learning is like. It's almost like a cognitive learning question. It's a way of getting at how you learn.

Andy: Let me ask you this. What if you answer this prompt and "go deep" the way you're describing BUT there's nothing related to this interest on your activities sheet or the list of extracurricular activities. Could that be a red flag to the admissions officer?

Sarah: For this prompt in particular? No. Not at all, no.

Andy: Okay.

Sarah: I actually prefer that. That reminds me of, was it the first prompt that says ... Yeah, so like if you have an interest or a talent that's really special to you but doesn't come up anywhere else so you want to talk about it here. I think it's the same thing. I think that's actually really great because it means that you're a multi-dimensional human with lots of different interests. Plus, I mean, the extracurriculars that are available to you are often determined by totally arbitrary things, like what your high school has historically had, what they can fund, who's interested in forming a club. That doesn't necessarily have to dictate or define what you love.

I like to see that people who are athletes, but also love music. Or people who write but also, I don't know, camp, do things in the outdoors. I think it's interesting because it shows that you're a little bit more multi-dimensional and again, it comes down to this question of what kind of a community member will you be at the school. Are you willing to take in new things, learn new things, contribute in new ways to the school community? Join clubs or start new clubs? Keep the campus life going, basically? That doesn't necessarily have to come down to what your formal extracurriculars are.

I used to say this all the time. At UChicago we didn't really have a formal equestrian organization. Nothing really horsey, but there are a lot of people who are really into equine activities, right? Being involved in that is still a good thing because it shows what kind of a person you are that you're active and involved and committed and passionate. Yeah, I don't think that they have to line up at all, and often it's better and more interesting if they don't.

> **Tip: This is your opportunity to "Nerd out" about an interest to demonstrate that you are curious and the lengths you go to learn. It does NOT have to relate to any of your extracurricular activities or anything else on your application!**

COLLEGE ADMISSIONS WEBCLASS

On a recent webcast, we worked through a case study on two shy, introverted kids who didn't know what to do to stand out on the college applications. Spoiler alert: they figured it out big time, so much so that they received a text from their Ivy League admissions officer congratulating them on how much their applications stood out in a crazy-competitive year! Here's where to see what we did:

www.CollegeAdmissionsWebcast.com

Chapter 9

Prompt 7

Share an essay on any topic of your choice. It can be one you've already written, one that responds to a different prompt, or one of your own design.

Andy: This prompt is new, it disappeared from the Common App for a couple of years but now it's back.

Sarah: Yeah. I mentioned UChicago always included a "write your own" prompt as well. I think it can be done well, but honestly, I think it can be a little bit of also an opportunity to trip yourself up a little. Like if you're obviously repurposing an essay you've already written. And it invites that.

Andy: Yeah![7]

Sarah: If you submit your 10th grade Honors English paper about *The Scarlet Letter* as your Common App essay, that tells the reader virtually nothing about you. I mean, probably everyone in your class was assigned the same essay, right? If you're going to choose the prompt, I think you should still write something original for it. If that means coming up with a prompt of your own that doesn't necessarily fit any of these, I think that's fine. You should definitely really make

---

[7] My god, what insight!

sure, though, before you do that, that it absolutely does not fit any of the above six prompts, which ...

Andy: It's almost like you have to go out of your way to avoid one of the first six, which are so open-ended. Personally, I think It's nice to have a little focus, so I would love everyone use this prompt as a last resort, only.

Sarah: Yeah, exactly, because I think you can really dig yourself in a hole with this. If you end up writing something where it's clear that all you're doing is trying to really brag about something in a kind of disingenuous, indirect way, and you create a prompt just so that you could brag about that thing, we all know what you're doing.

I think if you're going to choose this, you should still choose a good prompt that isn't covered by the above six. I would not encourage repurposing, especially a school essay or something like this because again, like I said, these are not the kind of essays most people usually write. I find it hard to imagine that anyone would have written something for class that would be really appropriate as a Common App essay.

Andy: Okay. I had a hard time seeing how one of the other ones would not be appropriate. I think back when they originally had this prompt there were fewer other choices.

Sarah: Six is a lot already!

Andy: Yeah. I think last year there were five total and now there's seven.

Sarah: Yeah.

Andy: I don't know, so it's ... I don't know what the increase is in response to, overall though I think I like the changes.

Sarah: Yeah, I do too. I do too.

Andy: OK, now let's go to some questions that came in from workshop registrants.

Tip: Don't answer this prompt. OK, seriously, think twice before tackling this choice, because the first six prompts are going to be adequate options 99.99% of the time. If you DO use this prompt, try not to make it obvious that the only reason you did so was to brag about yourself.

Chapter 10

Humor And The College Essay

Andy: All right, so let me fire away with some questions submitted before this webinar, and then I'm going to get to the chat and then we'll wrap up here. Question number one is about humor. This is from Michelle Russo. *Is it okay to use humor? Does it come across as cocky? Can it come across another way?* What are your thoughts on humor?

Sarah: I love humor. It can be diverting and refreshing. *If* that's a natural way of writing for you, if you're a funny person and you like to joke around and that's your natural voice. It's way better to hear your natural voice than something that's stilted and forced, because if you you normally would write like that but don't for this essay, then you might end up with something that's a little bit more generic that doesn't really sound like you.

If, on the other hand, you think you're supposed to be funny -- we see this a lot with the UChicago prompts especially -- if you think you're supposed to be funny but you're not normally funny, don't force it.

I think as with anything else humor can be deployed extremely well and can add some kind of a lightness and a levity to what is otherwise a very serious process for for all parties involved. Yeah, if you can make it a little fun and that's your way of doing it, then I think that's awesome and it'll communicate. Just like with anything else, again, know your audience, be sensitive to the potentially diverse audience that's reading your essay, and don't be, if you're worried that it's coming across as arrogant, it probably is. Soften it.

Andy: Yeah, well you wouldn't even be worried about it if you are arrogant, right?

Sarah: Right, exactly. That's very true.

Andy: But there's different types of humor, right? I mean, there's self-deprecating humor, which I think is almost always a win, and then there's also humor at the expense of others or like you were hinting at directed toward different minority groups or something like that, so some jokes work, some don't.

Sarah: Yeah, exactly. Self-deprecating is great because it shows that you have a lot of self-awareness and that's always an appealing quality in this process. The more self-awareness you can show, the better. Yeah, it's like the comedy rule, right? Number one, don't punch down. Don't do that.

Andy: All right, that's great. Okay, so I hope that helps. That was a great question from Michelle.

Chapter 11

Should You Talk About A Mental Illness Or Other Disability (Or Will That Backfire)?

Andy: Alright, this next question, *If a student has struggled with a mental illness like depression or bipolar disorder, is that something that works against them in disclosing it on an essay?*

Sarah: No, and I actually think it's really important to, if you're comfortable doing it and telling a story about it in some way, and if it's not being disclosed with your permission by your guidance counselor or another recommender in your letters of recommendation, which often times that does happen also. If it's not being disclosed there or talked about, it is helpful to hear about because then if the school chooses to admit you, that helps them know how to work with and accommodate you or to begin to think about those things. That way when you arrive to campus it's not a surprise for everyone, which means they'd be a little bit behind in figuring out how to accommodate you or to work with you. It's really just a way of helping the school a little bit better, just a kind of communication.

No, I don't think it's detrimental at all. I think it's a part of your story, if that is a part of your story. It's important for the school to know so that they can help work with you.

Andy: Yeah, I think a lot of people use it in the context of overcoming an obstacle type of essay prompt. For me, a lot of times when I talk to kids and some disability or something has been such a huge part of their life, to me it'd be a little incongruent or odd to NOT include that.

But then the question is, will doing so hurt my chances of getting admitted?

Can it ever hurt someone?

Sarah: No. I think it would be very rare that would. It would have to be in combination with other things that would already be hurting your application. That's a good point that you just brought up, which is that if for instance, the rigor of your coursework was slightly decreased than it otherwise might have been, or you took summer courses, or your grades were a little bit lower for a year or two than they otherwise might have been because you were dealing with a mental illness or some other disability, then that's extremely useful for your admissions officer to know, because that provides context for the academic record, which otherwise kind of sits there unexplained in and of itself, just isolated numbers or letters on a piece of paper.

I think actually the more context the better and I think that's absolutely right that if that is a major part of your story then yeah, it would almost be, incongruent is a good word, that's leaving out a massive piece of that story. Whether it applies to your academic record or your level of extracurriculars, the things you could participate in, or just your level of maturity or understanding of yourself, I think that can be important to know. It's obviously a very personal choice and I think it depends on your own level of dealing with it, willingness or readiness to speak about it, and to what degree. I would also be sure you include some information about your current state in managing your mental illness or disability so that the college has that information in hand.

There's also an additional information section of the common application that's much shorter, so I think you can kind of use that however you see fit, but I wouldn't worry about it hurting you. It's actually must more helpful than hurtful.

Andy: All right good, that always comes up so I'm glad you helped put that to rest.

Chapter 12

Should You Write About A Failed Relationship?

Andy: This question comes from Patricia. ***Should you stay away from writing about a failed relationship?***

Sarah: Yes. Sorry. Yeah, please don't write about love stuff. I had a colleague who was brilliant and she used to say that, and it's kind of the best, most succinct way to say it. Just stay away from the love stuff. In not even a year, in like six months, if you write that and submit it, you're going to look back and be like, "That's so embarrassing." That's not the kind of personal we really want to see. There are certain levels of intimacy that you just kind of don't necessarily need to see.

I think there are ways of writing about it, but it's so hard to distance yourself from that kind of a thing. There's a fine line between diary journal and narrative autobiography. You're shooting more for the latter and not the former and I think it's really hard just to write about a failed relationship and not write about it in those diary-like terms. I would avoid it. I'm sorry.

Andy: Yeah, so I read that question, I wasn't even sure that's what she was asking, which just shows how, I don't know, how unemotional I am!

Sarah: Andy's like, "What failed relationships, ever?"

Andy: No, no, i was thinking that "relationship" could be a father/son, it could be two friends, it could be anything that's not a love relationship.

Sarah: Okay, then you're right. If that is the case ... I was interpreting that as meaning romantic relationship. If it's about a romantic relationship, yes, I would stay away from it. If it's about a strained relationship or broken relationship with a friend or a relative or a loved one in any other terms then yes, I've read a lot of essays like that that can be pulled off very well. Yeah, the love stuff I would just, I'd stay away from. Sorry everyone.

Andy: Don't apologize for that one. I think you just helped a lot of people!

56

Chapter 13

Should You Choose The Least Common Prompt Because It's Least Common?

Andy: All right, this is a question from Martin, who's a current client. *Since question four (a problem you've solved or problem you'd like to solve) was written about the least, does that mean that you as an admissions officer might like reading that more because it's less popular?*

Sarah: Yeah, I think so. I think every time a prompt comes up that is not often responded on, there is a little prick of like, "Oh, this is interesting," but the prick can die very quickly if the essay is not very engaging. I would say yes, I think that can give you a very tiny bit of capital, but you have to do something with it in order for that to really mean anything in the end. It still has to be a good essay, basically.

Chapter 14

Should You Freak Out About The Essays (How Much Do They Count)?

Andy: Okay, I feel like everyone is asking themselves this question from Amy, who wants to know, ***Is anyone else freaking out about all this***?

What do you think? Should people freak out about the essay? How much does it really count?

Sarah: There's nothing I can say that will prevent probably anybody from freaking out during this process because it's mega stressful, I know that.

What I can say is that this is not about "gaming the system," even though I think that's what a lot of people look for, but in reality, what admissions officers enjoy reading is the opposite of that: actual genuineness and originality.

The fun thing about originality is that the way that we use it colloquially now means something else, but originality just means original, as in no one else has anything like it. Again, the great thing about that is that's who you are as a person.

Each individual person is unique. If you kind of really allow yourself to embrace that and sink into that and draw on that, and allow yourself to express yourself more personally and more intimately and more fearlessly in that way, then you're actually circumventing this whole insane rat race of like, "I have to say this and this and this, and be this and this and this." It doesn't work. There is no one thing. We don't know what we want to see until we see it. It's not like we prefer people who do this over this, or write this way over this way, or funny over serious. That's not how we think.

Andy: I feel like there's a lot of kids who wish they had cured cancer or built a village in a third world country or stuff like that, whereas, if I had to guess, I'd say 98% of kids applying to college have not done those monumental things.

Sarah: Yeah.

Andy: Sometimes parents feel like that's an issue for their kid and what I'm hearing you say is that's probably not an issue.

Sarah: Yeah, absolutely. Absolutely. It would be a ridiculous expectation to think that everyone has to have done something amazing in their lives by eighteen. The whole point is that you show potential, but you're applying to college so that you can get to college to get the skills to actually do those amazing things. You shouldn't have the expectation that you have to cure cancer just to get into college, right?

I think that the stress can often be misplaced in trying to figure out "what's my hook, what's the best thing that I can do, how can I present myself in a certain way?" But really I think the attention and energy is better placed on: "how can I break down all these weird barriers I have about writing about myself in a narrative and thoughtful and honest way?" That's a way better use of your energy.

Chapter 15

How Important Is The "Opening Line?"

Andy: All right, good. All right, a couple more questions then we'll wrap up here. I'm trying to focus on the ones I think are going to be good for the whole group. This a very good one from Ryan. ***How important are the opening lines of your essay?*** In terms of getting your attention.

Sarah: That's a really good question, Ryan. I think it just depends. I mean, a really good opening line can be quickly wasted on an otherwise lackluster essay, and a pretty lackluster couple of opening lines can otherwise be redeemed by a great essay.

I think that probably the more important thing is that if your opening line or opening lines show clarity and intention and focus, then that's going to help drive the reader's attention forward. I don't think it's so much about grabbing them and pulling them in, because in reality that's just very hard to do and very few adult writers can do that. It's more about showing honestly the results of fine editing and focus in your writing so that I have confidence in reading it that you're taking me somewhere.

Andy: Sarah, if you have 800 to 1,000 applications to review, including their essays and supplemental essays and all that, when you get an essay like we're talking about that clearly signals to you the benefit to you of why you should read that essay, I think that's got a better shot at being read by you in a good mood, right?

Sarah: Yeah. I mean, absolutely. Everything does get read, but I think some things get read more begrudgingly than others, right? Some things are a lot more fun to read.

Andy: Yeah.[8]

Sarah: I think it's not so much the content of the opening lines that you need to worry about or focus on or belabor over. It's more the style of them, and to show the discernment and the editing process. Demonstrating that there's focus and clarity. If it's a rambling first sentence that very clearly shows it has no direction, it's like, oh my God, the whole essay's going to be like this.

Show intention. Cut out adverbs and adjectives.

---

[8] Another grand slam! Shrewd commentary like this is worth the price of this book alone.

Chapter 16

What To Do If You're "Not A Good Writer" Or Suffer From "College Essay Writer's Block"

Andy: Oh great. I'm going to combine two questions here. This is partially from Karen. *What tips do you have for a more techy-minded student who may not be the best essay writer?" Or anyone in general who is not a "good writer". Is that person at a disadvantage?*

Sarah: That's a really good question. I ended up working with a lot of more STEM-oriented kids last year. What I actually find is that kids across all areas of interest and disciplines can be good writers and also less good writers. I think it almost depends more on how they think, how much they think, and how much they read, honestly. I've not done this before, but now that it's occurring to me, it would not be a bad idea to encourage students who are not maybe right out the gate super comfortable with their writing, to read a little bit more going into this essay-writing process. Just read good writing, read things that move them, whether it's fiction or nonfiction, because I think they spend a lot more time, especially the latter half of high school, reading textbooks, right? That's maybe a little bit less interesting. If they can kind of get you in the mind and get the creative juices flowing, I think that's helpful. [*Note from Sarah*: I really recommend long form pieces in *The New Yorker* for this. They're much longer than anything you'll write in an application, but they're a master class in taking a massive amount of information and telling a compelling, clearly written, driven yet nuanced story.]

Also, the same rules apply from before. The person reading it doesn't expect everybody to be an amazing prose writer. That's just unrealistic and it would not be fair. Some people have a natural facility for it, but the people who are ready for MFA programs should not be privileged in this process just because they happen to be zippy writers. That's not usually how it works.

Yes, it does make the reading process a little bit more pleasurable, but it also means you have to keep in mind that some students are just not going to write that way. I think you can trust your admissions officer to know that and to give you the benefit of the doubt and also, try to get a little bit more comfortable writing more personally. If it helps to focus on concrete details, I find that actually can help things along a little bit.

Ask yourself these questions consciously. How did it feel? What did I say? How did I react? Those kinds of things. They won't necessarily all make it in, but it'll put you in the mood.

Andy: Yeah, listen, that's great advice. I've seen seen kids who consider themselves to be good writers and they just fall in love with their own writing and they fill up their pages with all sorts of flowery, multi-syllabic words that feel like they swallowed a thesaurus, that type of thing.

I'm like, "Yeah, I know you're a good writer, okay, but not everyone agrees with you.

I've also seen, particularly for STEM types, kids who have something to say but they don't know where to start. They have College Essay Writer's Block.

I say, "Look, sometimes I feel like the best essays are written almost conversationally. Cleaned up of course!

Why don't you just outline it and then just talk it through, record it transcribe it, and then edit it from there?" Sometimes that's a really quick way for people to get unstuck, to relieve themselves from college essay writers block and it turns out to be a very readable essay

Sarah: Yeah, that's actually a really great idea. That's something that lot of writers I think try to do themselves, just kind of barf ou something on paper, assuming that no one has to see it but you an God, and then you can edit it as many times as you need to to get it t a good point, but just to break that barrier down that you have abou writing.

Also, to your first point, that's absolutely true and I think students wh really like to write creatively can also write mediocre essays for tha exact reason, right? Too in love with their own prose. I think th advantage in that case that more STEM-oriented or research-oriented students might have is actually that they think more for clarity an more for focus and more for intention and more for getting to th point. Maybe a lot less likely to use unnecessary adverbs an adjectives and sentence clauses and things that are going to muddle u the point, and more likely to see clearly what the point is and to ge you there, right?

That's what I want. That's all I want when I'm reading! Guys, I jus want someone to take my hand and be like, "I know where we'r going. It's a beautiful place. Let me just take you down this path, and like, oh look, wasn't that painless and beautiful? Now it's over." Have the confidence to lead. That's all I want.

Chapter 17

How To Conclude An Essay

Andy: All right, so the final question, which is actually very appropriate, is ***What concluding lines should be written at the end of an essay?*** That's a hard question to answer.

Sarah: That's such a hard question. I think that's often the thing that kids struggle with the most. That's something I struggle with the most. Okay, there isn't one particular thing obviously that you can write that's going to be better than others, but what I will say is this. Do not waste precious, precious word count words to wind down to the conclusion for like a paragraph and a half. Right?

Andy: By the way, sorry to interrupt, we did get a couple questions about that. The maximum is 650 words.

Sarah: 650 is actually quite short for a lot of people for what they want to say. You're going to have to cut down a lot. When I'm reading and when I'm working with students, this comes up for me a lot. Every single thing that goes in there should be important. If you're wasting words on useless sentences or things that don't get you anywhere or have no purpose, or three sentences of conclusion when you really only needed a sentence, that says to me that maybe there just wasn't enough substance otherwise to go into the thing.

Andy: Right.

Sarah: You don't ever want to lead your reader into that potentia conclusion. It should be active, active, active all the way to the end. Everything in it should be doing work. One concluding sentence is actually fine.

Andy: I feel like a lot of times it's almost like the essays conclude themselves because they are so short. People sometimes say, "Wow, 650. That's kind of a lot."

It's actually two pages plus, it's not that long. I think it's a lot harder to write a short essay than it is like a 10-pager because you have to only include the stuff that's going to tell your story and remove all the fluff, so that's why you don't need a whole conclusionary paragraph in my experience.

Sarah: Yeah, exactly. That is what's challenging about this. I think you're right, that you have to kill your darlings. You're going to write something the first time through that's way longer than you need. Almost everyone does and you have to have the discipline to cut the things that you like a lot, because they're your own writing.

But you've got to be willing to sacrifice. Something that I ended up doing a lot last year was saying, "What is the backbone? Trace the spine of this story that you're telling throughout the essay." It should follow the prompt. We saw that over and over again. The prompt gives you the arch of the story that it wants, so you follow the prompt, identify what the spine of the story is, what the shape is, and anything that isn't really helping to tell that story or contributing, it's got to go. Gotta kill it. Take it out.

Andy: That's great. Every sentence. Every sentence needs to support that somehow.

Sarah: Yeah, it all has to serve a purpose. It's all got to pull its weight and if it's not pulling any kind of weight, even if it's beautiful, even if it's Ernest Hemingway, sorry.

Andy: The cliché is, "There's no such thing as good writing, there is good rewriting."

Sarah: Yeah, absolutely. Yeah. I really believe that.

Chapter 18

Actual Essays

For "Inspiration," not "Blatant Ripping Off"

I've chosen to share these essays because each of them is interesting. And each writer was admitted to his or her top choice colleges (including a few Ivies) and, in many cases, received a hefty amount of scholarships.

I want you to notice how our clients dealt with overcoming obstacles, "went small," surprised the reader and used humor, among other things. You'll also note minor grammatical or stylistic gaffes; they're included to demonstrate that you do not have to submit a Pulitzer Prize winner.

Final note: I'm trusting that you will not plagiarize these. If you do, I will hunt you down and call you mean names (I can be quite harsh!) until you admit your transgression to whatever colleges admitted you because of your copycatting. So there.

So there I was standing on the steps of Capitol Hill, home of the legislative branch of the United States of America, with a frog in my throat and beads of sweat running down my forehead. My first meeting was scheduled for 1:00 p.m., and I would be seeing New York State Senators Charles Schumer and Kirsten Gillibrand, and Congressman Steve Israel. I was in Washington D.C., on behalf of the Epilepsy Foundation of America. In 2013, I started working with the Epilepsy Foundation's Teen Council to raise awareness, eradicate the stigma of seizure disorders, and raise funds for their local community programs. The goal was to better the lives of those with epilepsy.

I was diagnosed with a seizure disorder when I was eleven years old and spent four years hiding it from everyone. While others talked about what spring or winter vacation they had taken here or there, I listened quietly hoping no one would ask me: my breaks almost always involved a three day stint in the hospital for an extended EEG. Nobody could really understand what it was like to be me. Each day I dreaded the public humiliation of a seizure and privately dealt with the embarrassment and shame.

By my junior year, I felt further alienated as each of my classmates passed their driving tests and it became increasingly difficult to be happy for others while I secretly resented their excitement. I woke up one morning and decided that I was tired of pretending that my life was just like everyone else's - it just wasn't. Although it was liberating to finally tell others, many students were taken aback. I had played soccer all my life, run track, played in the school band, and made honor roll - yet some of my peers thought that epilepsy was a form of mental retardation. I knew more awareness was needed, and I wanted to do something to help others; I just wasn't exactly sure what one fifteen year old could do to change the world's perception of what it was like to live with epilepsy.

I was nominated by the Epilepsy Foundation of Long Island to represent them in Washington D.C., and underwent intensive public speaking and advocacy training. I went to lobby congress for support of pending drug patent laws and to ask for a $15 million increase to the Center for Disease Control's budget for neurological research. I explained to the Senators and Congressman that I had no traumatic brain injury, no viral or bacterial infection, nor any family history of epilepsy. How could doctors effectively treat my epilepsy if they didn't have any idea why my brain was malfunctioning? Increased funding to the CDC for research could lead to new breakthroughs in treatment, and new treatments were desperately needed.

I described how my first medication affected my liver and my hair started to fall out. A second, newer, drug caused such debilitating nausea that I lost 30 pounds in 4 months. The third drug made me so tired and confused that it interfered with my memory and cognitive function. I brought my pill box filled with one day's antiepileptic regimen: three different anti-epileptics for a total of 28 pills. I discussed the alarming statistics with each of the members of Congress and respectfully asked for their support. It was a proud moment for me as I had always had difficulty discussing this very private side of my life. By the time I left, I had their word that they would sponsor both causes.

Ultimately, the pending bills did not pass, but I hope that they will be passed someday in my lifetime. I feel that living with this disability has helped me to understand that it is important to stand up for what you believe in. I have struggled over the past four years, and I've come very close to giving up. However, I have realized that life isn't about what you don't have or what you can't do – it's about being grateful for what you do have and making the most of your strengths. I am a person living with epilepsy, but I am not an epileptic; I refuse to let it define who I am. As I left at the end of that day, I paused on the stairs and turned to look back at the building: it wasn't just a critically important building where law-making took place, it was the place where I had found the courage to speak out for what I believed in, and it was the last stop on an amazing odyssey for me.

Andy's two cents: THIS is an essay about overcoming a real obstacle. Instead of making excuses and asking for the reader to feel sorry for him, the writer tells the story of his journey in an inspirational - and interesting - way!

"I haven't wiped since October!" my Dad shouted. We were in a crowded restaurant, out with another family. My friend looked up from her dessert in shock and disgust. But I keep eating, as if nothing happened. The funny thing is, I wasn't even remotely embarrassed by this comment.

My dad was bragging again about his new gadget, the "Toto Toilet," which basically does everything -EVERYTHING- for you. (It is like a car wash for your backside, you don't need to know any more). My Dad, the enthusiastic, unfiltered guy.

My Dad is my role model for passion and enthusiasm, he has inspired me to put full effort into anything and everything I do. Since I was 12, I have swum six days a week for two hours a day. Every morning at five o'clock I hear the agonizing sound of my alarm, slowly roll over to shut it and get out of bed. I change (but put my pajamas on over my swimsuit), grab my banana and coffee and wake up my Mom to drive me.

My Mom constantly marvels that I don't have to be harassed to wake up. Don't get me wrong, I love sleep as much as any other teenager, there are many mornings when I question myself, weighing my options of staying under my warm covers. But my passion for swimming and competition drags me out of bed each time.

My Dad and I share an extreme devotion to our team, The New York Mets. Since I was five, every August 25th, the day before my birthday, my Dad and I would go to a game. We see many games together, but if I am not at Citi Field, I am watching at home, or receiving live updates on my phone, always with my official Mets ballcap on, because it's good luck, obviously!

During critical moments my heart beats faster, I clench my fists, and shout "C'mon!" (and, depending on the outcome, other words that I prefer not to share in print). I spend hours researching players' statistics and catching up on breaking team news. My friends may binge on Netflix, I am glued to Sports center and ESPN.

My drive reveals itself in other, more important ways, such as helping others. When my grandmother was diagnosed with cancer, I spent days and weeks in the hospital with her. On each visit I also met other cancer patients of all ages. Seeing the patients and hearing all their stories affected me deeply, and made me realize how no one deserves this terrible experience.

I decided that I needed to do something to make their treatment even the slightest bit more enjoyable. After my grandmother passed away, I started a foundation in her name to comfort other cancer patients. I dealt with tedious legal and accounting paperwork, I spent hours upon hours designing a website, and months finding outreaches, donors, and knitters for the gifts we create, which I continue to do. There have been many times where my friends have asked me to go out on Friday and Saturday nights, but, frequently, I force myself to stay in and catch up on this work. This experience has shown me that I can harness my passion in important areas other than fun and games.

I am excited for what the future has in store. I am looking forward to college and being able to explore more about myself and the world around me, and find even more to become enthusiastic about. I'm eager to experience all nighters, meet new people and throw myself into new extracurricular and volunteer opportunities.

I know that there will be times where I will be utterly exhausted, but I also know that the enthusiasm that I inherited from my Dad will keep me going long after my friends and I are "wiped" out!

Andy's two cents: My favorite essay from last year's crop. The dad wanted to title it, "Ode To The Commode," which, thankfully, he suggested long after his daughter submitted this to her top choice choice college, got in and received a $25,000 per year scholarship!

I love this opening line, a real attention-grabber, but the best part of this essay is that it's not about a toilet - it's about the writer's passion and enthusiasm.

And, seriously, can you imagine an admissions officer reading it? It's so different and interesting, they must have been FLUSH with excitement to review it!

As a child, I was under the impression that adults have it all figured out. They know the answer to any question you ask with such convincing certainty. They have the skills to handle dangerous tasks, like using the stove and driving a car. Their seemingly effortless way of knowing the right thing is intimidating. They understand things about life that your little child brain can't comprehend just yet. "But wait, don't worry," I thought, "because when you get older, you'll magically transform into an adult, too. Just wait and See!"

It turns out I was very wrong.

When faced with the question of identifying my transition from a child to an adult, my initial response was, "Don't you have to be an adult to answer that?" Although I do my own laundry, pay for my own movie tickets, and have my own job, I'm only a high school student who lives at home with my parents; definitely not an adult.

But what really makes someone an official "adult" and how do you become one? For much of my life, including my childhood, I've prided myself on my "adult-like" attributes: mature, responsible, accountable, capable. Being respected by my family, teachers, and friends has always been rewarding, making me feel that I had a head start on my way to adulthood.

When it comes to these characteristics of being an adult, I don't believe I made a transition, because I've always possessed these mature qualities. Sure, I loved playing with Polly Pockets and watching Nickelodeon as much as the next kid. But even since the 2nd grade, when homework started being assigned, my parents never had to make sure I was doing it. Whenever they did ask me about homework, my response would always be, "Guys, I've got this, don't worry." Having a no-nonsense attitude my whole life, I've always been aware of how the world works, rarely being fooled by childish fallacies. Because of the close relationship I have with my older sister, I've known from a young age that the world doesn't revolve around me, and that other people's views and perceptions are always important to consider.

There is no single instant or moment of complete change that occurs. It's a never ending journey with no tangible "final destination." Even when we get older and have more life experience, we continue to grow and transform continuously making our way to adulthood. Although some people may be more mature than others, no one can truly say that they're perfect with no room for positive change. There's no magical age or experience that you go through and instantly transform into an adult. Rather it's a perpetual process that's not meant to have an end. Unlike my childish assumption, adults don't have everything figured out, which is why it's necessary to continually grow and change.

As a 17 year old, I'm capable of handling a stove and driving a car. I can answer a lot of history and math questions with convincing certainty. I have natural authority over the campers at my summer job. And yet, even though I possess these adult qualities, I still don't feel like an adult. Despite my maturity, I don't have it all figured out, and probably never will. My childhood idea of what it means to be an adult has stuck with me even into my teens despite the fact that I know it to be untrue. I don't believe that I'll really ever feel like a genuine adult. But, then again, who does?

Andy's two cents: This is a great example of an essay that turns the prompt on its head. The original prompt asked about a transition to adulthood, the writer of this essay answered it by explaining that she never really transitioned, she was always an "old soul."

My dad and I never play catch. As long as I have been alive, he always has had to walk with a cane and sometimes uses a wheelchair. Also after long periods of sitting down his legs become tight, making it harder than it already is for him to walk. Although we sometimes tried to play, it could not last more than a couple throws due to my father's inability to balance.

When he stumbled, I would immediately try to help him, but he would become frustrated, wishing he didn't need that kind of help or look weak in front of his son. Sometimes he would snap at me, which would make me feel angry, or sad. After all, I was just trying to help him without thinking anything of it.

Going on vacation as well is another trek in itself. At airports we always need to find someone to wheel my Dad through airport security and help him onto the plane. It would make me feel frustrated and depressed as I would watch him struggle with something so minor like going through airport security. But he never seemed to mind.

All of this was just the normal way of life for our family. As a child I didn't even realize there was a different way of living life and I was accepting of that. My Dad's inability to walk does not stop us from being together as a family and he never complains. Although it may be more difficult, we are still able to go on vacations, go out to eat and even visit amusement parks.

I remember a time when I was 10 or 11, all the Dads were to get together with their kids on the baseball field for little league. It was one day that was supposed to be one giant father- son game. I knew immediately, even at that young of an age, that there was no possible way of my Dad getting on the field to play ball. At first I felt embarrassed, even ashamed. I then became angry with myself, there was nothing my Dad could do to fix the situation, it wasn't his choice.

I've taken care of my father for as long as I can remember. I actually enjoy it and feel good about myself, even though I don't always do the best job. When my Mom goes to work I cook for us I since my dad cannot stand up long enough to do so. But the first time I attempted to cook, I made chicken cutlets. I thought that they turned out okay, until my mom came home from work and asked why I felt the need to cook everything on high, since she almost lost a tooth biting into the meal I prepared.

At first, I got angry and frustrated, none of my friends had to cook, why did I? Gradually, however, I came to realize that I should appreciate the ability to do everyday tasks, given that my father is unable to do so. Taking care of him helped me grow up, since I started to think more about him, instead of focusing on my feelings.

It is hard to fully understand what he is going through on a day to day basis given that I don't suffer from his disease. I admit that it is still disheartening for me to see my dad in this condition, but the example he sets for me, being optimistic and positive, inspires me every day in a way that my friends' fathers cannot.

Andy's two cents: This is a terrific essay that uses the flip side of a common, Norman Rockwell-esque father-son activity of playing catch - that we can all relate to - to illustrate that things were different in the writer's childhood. Instead of being a depressing, sad essay, the writer describes how his father's health struggles inspired him to do his best. And got into almost every college he applied to, and received a huge scholarship from his top choice college! :)

I suppose most kids would feel most comfortable at their summer homes, or their room, or maybe a sports field, but my special place is behind a grill. As a founding member of the Staples Barbecue Club, the grill has become a second home for me, where all the day's stress can be forgotten in a juicy burger and washed down with a cool soda while at the same time treating others to the same medicine.

At home my parents are the bosses; they run their business and keep us kids in line, but this is not the case at our barbecues. Although we have a teacher advisor it is really the students who run the club. It is a place where I can work semi-independently with my peers and see what I'm really capable of.

In many ways Barbecue Club is a small business, so given my parent's background as small business owners, many of my friends look to me for leadership. I taught myself how to plan how many people are going to be at a barbecue, what kind of food are we going to buy, for what price, and how much will we sell it for. It is important to make money at each barbecue as the club funds itself with the money from the previous event. Just like any business in the real world.

When we took over the club in sophomore year, it was basically nonexistent. A teacher tried to get it started a couple years before but he and his students didn't even manage one barbecue. Still, my friends and I were determined to make Barbecue Club happen, so we went out and created relationships with our principal, the sports director and a local restaurant, who showed us some tricks for barbecuing and even gave us some free pulled pork with their secret recipe!

Of course not every business runs smoothly forever. For us this was the beginning of 2014 when we were visited by our new friends at the at the Health Department. It turned out that we were not following all of their criteria. They informed us that, until we fixed things, we wouldn't be allowed to barbecue. Even though no one had ever gotten sick at our barbecues, we understood the their concerns. Honestly, it would have been easier to shut things down, but no one wanted to abandon our club. So, we spent months taking food safety courses and rented a shack to prepare for next year's football season. It certainly put a blemish on our year, but we all pulled our weight and even managed to fit in one final barbecue!

The best thing about barbecue club is that it's a place that provides a real, genuine hangout. High school can stressful, but when I'm at a barbecue with my best friends, serving people and watching a football or soccer game, all the days worries drift away. We provide something that is disappearing from modern kid's lives. An unstructured hangout where you can see people face to face, instead of being on I-phones or goofing around online. I love video games just as much as most teenagers, but this is a different, better kind of fun. It's not just for kids, the principal and several of the vice principals love to attend the barbecues to enjoy the great food but they also get to connect with the students. If you see any of them in school they're usually busy and in a rush, but at one of our events they're just like anyone of us students: there to socialize and enjoy good food. Our barbecues bring the whole school closer together and make us a real community. I think of Barbecue Club as a place where everyone at the school can feel perfectly content, and am proud in the role I played to create it.

Andy's two cents: I think of this essay as a "slice of life" piece about something fun, but the writer uses it as a lens to describe some very important aspects of his personality and experiences that naturally resonated with the reader - he got into his top choice college!

My mom and I walked into the principal's office. He shook his head slowly and shut the door.

My crime? I had not stolen final exams, I was not accused of changing my grades.

Two nights earlier, I climbed into bed with a bowl of ice cream and logged onto my family computer. I was bored. The school year had ended and I couldn't bear to study for my finals. I considered my options: High School Musical? Minecraft? I logged on to Twitter.

My fellow middle school students were tweeting at our teachers. My wheels started turning. I thought it would be funny to open an account for my History teacher, Tom Curtin. I got the name @realmrcurtin123 (@realmrcurtin had already been taken?)

I tweeted for maybe an hour. Nothing bad. Just sayings of Mr.Curtin's and random opinions on World War II (his favorite American War). Other teacher accounts suddenly popped up, soon every teacher appeared to be tweeting. We chatted online as if we were teachers talking in a conference room. I logged off at 10:00.

The next morning I had 400 followers and 50 direct messages. During my English final the "Twitter Boom" was all anyone was talking about. My friends and I speculated who could be behind the joke. They didn't know it was me. I suggested some other kids.

Of course the principal found out what happened. About 100 kids in my grade were pulled away for interviews in the middle of finals. I was not one of them. I thought I had gotten away with it.

I went home and told my parents about this hilarious prank, but I omitted mentioning my involvement. I thought I fooled them.

But it wasn't over. All parents received an email informing them that the police had been contacted and that the computers of those involved would be subpoenaed if confessions weren't made by noon the following day. A shiver went up my back.

My parents called me downstairs. "Ashley, are you sure you have nothing to do with this Twitter thing?"

"Oh my god! That's so insulting! Why would I be involved?" I ran upstairs, deactivated my account, shut the computer down and shoved it under my bed. As if that would help.

I sat on my floor in a sweat and considered throwing my computer in a dump. After 10 minutes, I tiptoed back down the steps. "Mom? Dad? I have a confession-"

Next thing I knew I was in the principal's office. "I'm @therealmrcurtin123!" I started to cry.

I wasn't allowed to march in graduation or permitted on the class trip. I served in school suspension for five days. I played with a unicorn puzzle and read the entire Diary of a Wimpy Kid series twice over.

On Day 3 or 4, Mr. Curtin appeared. I braced myself for the angry talk I knew I deserved. Instead, he actually told me that he was flattered to have had such an impact on me. Before he walked away, he said "Ashley, thank you for all the laughs."

I still think that what I did was not that bad in the grand scheme of things. That is not the point. I learned that "harmless" pranks can have unforeseen consequences. I stayed off social media for a year and didn't look at a single computer for the entire summer. I learned that what you put online can never be erased.

Perhaps worst of all, I have been unable to get through a single argument with my mother without her saying "don't think I'm over the Twitter incident!"

Andy's two cents: I was around when this happened to the writer in 8th grade and, after it occurred, I immediately asked the dad:

1. *Can your daughter be my social media intern?*

2. *Great college essay!*

Dad told me "too early" for Question 1., but the answer to Question 2 became self-evident! The writer narrates the story about a transgression that was extremely serious at the time, but, upon reflection, is able to make a little fun of herself and draw an important lesson from it.

She got into her top choice college too!

Chapter 19

College Essay Prompts I'd Like To See

I wrote this next piece in 2015 as a blog post, recently uncovered it, started reading and immediately giggling to myself. I'm including it in this book because I hope you'll find it amusing and honestly have no idea what else to do with it.

The Common App essay prompts were officially released August 1 and they have been confounding college-bound teens all summer.

Why? They're ANNOYING!

And hard to write. And did I mention annoying?

How many kids do you know who overcame a serious challenge or obstacle that's worth bragging about to someone they haven't met but who can affect their future?

I'm sick of these questions, so instead of complaining, I thought I'd offer some essay prompts I'd like to see.

1. "Diversity" means different things to different people. Students at _____ University hail from all kinds of social, ethnic, economic and religious backgrounds. How much money does your family have? Describe, rounded to the nearest $10,000, your parents' income, their savings accounts, and fully discuss their ability to pay your tuition,

giving special consideration to their likelihood to voluntarily donate to our endowment during and after your years with us.

2. It is said that we are bombarded by more than 5,000 unique messages each day, and our ability to sort through these messages critically is essential to becoming a successful citizen and contributor to today's global community. How easily influenced by our marketing are you? Your answer may include, but should not be limited to: our tsunami of "personal," deceptive emails, our glossy brochures depicting a melting pot of acne-free, smiling college students of all races and creeds, our athletic teams' results, our Five Diamond dining options and luxury, spa-like living conditions. Your answer need not include graduation rates or success of our graduates finding jobs that actually pay bills.

3. "Ah, to write, that is to breathe..to search, to live!" We just made that quote up. But it sounds like some pretentious saying that could be googled within 1.7 seconds and used in a supplemental essay. Describe your search for the perfect College Essay Consultant, and how your parents ultimately decided to hire her or him to ghostwrite your essays. Example: If your folks interviewed middle-aged moo-moo wearing hippie poets who serve as adjunct professors at a local college and live with more than five cats, elaborate on your personal search. If you met with any consultant that implicitly or expressly indicated that, because they have written essays for other people who got into Yale, you too will be admitted to Yale, please indicate how much you paid them.

4. Most colleges would brag that their campuses are examples of the culture of ideas, where free debate and diversity of opinion are welcomed and encouraged. Yet, approximately 90% of professors are

registered members of one political party. Please help us square these contradictory facts, because we cannot (or are unwilling to).

5. Suck up to us in 250 words or less.

Resources

Below are resources that can help you with the college admissions, financial aid and scholarships process. There's a mixture of free, nearly free and not free stuff here.

Webinar on creating a game plan for college admissions strategies, how to choose colleges that will actually help your kid succeed post-college, scholarships: www.CollegeAdmissionsWebcast.com

Webinar on financial aid formulas, loopholes, land mines: www.FinancialAidWebcast.com

How To Pay "Wholesale" For College. Best-selling book on financial aid strategies for "Forgotten Middle Class" families. Available on Amazon.

The Incomparable Applicant. Best-selling book on how to stand out to an admissions officer when you have the same grades and standardized test scores as 5,000 other competitor-applicants. Available on Amazon.

Financial Aid Forms Prep Service: www.CollegeGuruAcademy.com. Fast, easy, accurate and on-time preparation of your FAFSA, CSS Profile and other forms.

Rev.com - the transcription service I referred to re: the advice for those afflicted with College Essay Writer's Block. (I suggested outlining, dictating, recording and transcribing. I used Rev for a big chunk of this book!)

On Writing The College Application Essay - Harry Bauld. Originally written in the 1980's, I've read and re-read this book on a practically annual basis since I got into the college planning field more than 16 years ago. I can't recommend it enough. Available on Amazon last time I checked.

Private college coaching services from us: Call the office, 516-882-5464 or email us, VIP@andylockwood.com. Available for qualified local, out-of-state and international students.

Testimonials

I know a lot of college planners who promise results but don't deliver. In your case, I got real results.

- Dr. Dennis O'Hara
Superintendent, Hauppauge School District

Nicole is at her dream school, got her Presidential Scholarship - $25K! Thank you for all your help. I always recommend you to my friends. You and your team played a great role during that painful process. Thank god it's over lol!

- Elina Kazakevich, Staten Island NY

I needed someone to bounce ideas off of for the essays, it was great to have you. I knew my English teachers could not help me. Thank you!

- Julia Petrini, Brown University

Thank you for all your help throughout the entire challenging process, esp. with the applications and essays!

-Victorien Jakobsen, Vassar College

We used Andy for the applications and essays. The whole thing was overwhelming, don't try this on your own! We will be back with our younger daughter.

- Joe Iannone
Owner, Avellino's Pizzeria
Garden City, NY

As soon as I walked through your door I felt as if a huge weight had been lifted off my shoulders. Thank you for all you have done for my precious girls!

-Beth Marcus, Scottsdale, AZ

Andy

You probably do not remember me but I came to one of your seminars at the Roslyn JCC and also took advantage of the free consultation at your office last year.

Unfortunately, the economic downturn combined with an extremely contentious divorce left me in a situation where I had basically no funds to pay for my son's tuition or to work with you. However, I remained on your email list and still received priceless information that was invaluable to my son's entire financial aid process. I can only imagine what you can do for the "paying customers."

My son was admitted to Tulane University and received an extremely generous aid package. I strongly believe that what i learned from your blasts was a big part of it. Thank you for providing this, and as my financial situation improves, I look forward to consulting with you in person for my other children.

I will be opting out of the email list, but surely will return in a couple of years.

Sincerely,
- M.F. [Name withheld by Andy]
Great Neck, NY

I came to see you after attending a workshop. You told me not to waste my money retaining you because you could not help me.

That's when I knew you were an honest man.

- Anthony DiBattista,
New Hyde Park, New York

The Weston High School PTO hosted Andy for an extremely informative and entertaining seminar on the best-kept secrets of securing the ideal financial aid package.

Weston is home to a high income parent population and most walked away not just pleased but astonished that they could, in fact, qualify for financial aid!

The PTO received terrific feedback and we are looking forward to having Andy back next year -- kudos to Andy for a job well done!

-- Lisa Bigelow
Vice President, Weston (CT) High School PTO

Andrew Lockwood, a college finance consultant, has conducted two classes at the South Huntington Public library. Each event was well attended and parents seemed to be very interested in the material presented. I would recommend that any library in an area with a significant population of college-bound children host a similar workshop with Mr. Lockwood.

Catherine Schmoller
Director of Public Relations & Adult Programming
South Huntington (NY) Library

Lisa, Please thank Andy Lockwood for his wonderful presentation at our recent Board Meeting. We found it very informative and helpful.

I am sure a lot of the parents who attended the presentation will be following up with him for subsequent meetings.

Thanks again,- Lisa Edelblum
President, Roslyn (NY) PTO

Book Andy to speak

Although financial aid isn't the most exciting topic, Andy does his best to make it and the college admissions process easy to understand, enjoyable and occasionally humorous (especially to himself).

However, thin-skinned, easily insulted and politically-correct groups should NOT invite him to speak, because Andy's presentations are blunt and opinionated and known to offend people wearing "Insult Antennae." Topics include:

- How to construct a college list *strategically* (not solely based on rear window stickers of cars driving around your neighborhood) - even if your son/daughter has "no clue" about they want to do with the rest of their lives

- How to get a jump on the FAFSA and other financial aid forms so you can get the most money you can possibly get

- Little-known legal & ethical "loopholes" that, if deployed properly, will save you big bucks!

- The most important question on the Common App...that isn't actually ON it but must be answered

- The inconvenient truth about what admissions officers are REALLY looking for in a candidate (hint: it ain't only about GPA and SAT/ACT scores)

- 3 deadly college essay mistakes and how to avoid them

- Divorced and separated families: WATCH OUT! How to navigate the forms

- The 529 - "Friend" or "Foe?" (and what to do if you have one)

- Special business owner "landmines" to avoid at all costs

- Case studies of kids who got into Ivy League and other super-competitive schools

If you're willing to risk YOUR reputation and standing in your community, contact Andy at the office, 516-882-5464 or via email, VIP@andylockwood.com

Made in the USA
Columbia, SC
12 August 2022

65242996R00059